My Life
What I Did Today

A Doggie Journal From MyDogCorner

My What I Did Today Doggie Journal

Copyright © 2019 MyDogCorner

All rights reserved.

ISBN: 9781093269987

DEDICATION

Dedicated to all of those that have a loved one waiting for them over the rainbow bridge. We always want more time with our furbabies. We hope keeping this journal will help you keep all the wonderful memories alive while you wait to meet with them again.

My Forever Home

First Address: _____

_____

The Welcoming Party: _____

_____

My First Toy: _____

My First Meal: _____

Signed With My Dirty Paw Print:

My First Days At Home

My Favorite Toy: _____

_____

My Personality Quirks: _____

_____

Where/How I Slept: _____

_____

Special Moments: _____

_____

_____

_____

What Happened Today

DATE: _____

NOTES:

_____
_____
_____
_____
_____
_____
_____
_____
_____
_____
_____
_____
_____

Photo Of The Day:

What Happened Today

DATE: _____

NOTES:

_____
_____
_____
_____
_____
_____
_____
_____
_____
_____
_____
_____
_____
_____
_____
_____

Photo Of The Day:

What Happened Today

DATE: _____

NOTES:

_____

_____

_____

_____

_____

_____

_____

_____

_____

_____

_____

_____

_____

Photo Of The Day:

What Happened Today

DATE: _____

NOTES:

_____
_____
_____
_____
_____
_____
_____
_____
_____
_____
_____
_____
_____
_____
_____
_____
_____

Photo Of The Day:

What Happened Today

DATE: _____

NOTES:

_____

Photo Of The Day:

What Happened Today

DATE: _____

NOTES:

_____
_____
_____
_____
_____
_____
_____
_____
_____
_____
_____
_____
_____
_____
_____
_____
_____
_____

Photo Of The Day:

What Happened Today

DATE: _____

NOTES:

_____

Photo Of The Day:

What Happened Today

DATE: _____

NOTES:

_____
_____
_____
_____
_____
_____
_____
_____
_____
_____
_____
_____
_____
_____
_____
_____
_____

Photo Of The Day:

What Happened Today

DATE: _____

NOTES:

Photo Of The Day:

What Happened Today

DATE: _____

NOTES:

_____
_____
_____
_____
_____
_____
_____
_____
_____
_____
_____
_____
_____
_____
_____
_____
_____

Photo Of The Day:

What Happened Today

DATE: _____

NOTES:

_____
_____
_____
_____
_____
_____
_____
_____
_____
_____
_____
_____
_____

Photo Of The Day:

What Happened Today

DATE: _____

NOTES:

_____
_____
_____
_____
_____
_____
_____
_____
_____
_____
_____
_____
_____
_____
_____

Photo Of The Day:

What Happened Today

DATE: _____

NOTES:

_____
_____
_____
_____
_____
_____
_____
_____
_____
_____
_____
_____
_____
_____

Photo Of The Day:

What Happened Today

DATE: _____

NOTES:

_____
_____
_____
_____
_____
_____
_____
_____
_____
_____
_____
_____
_____
_____
_____
_____
_____
_____

Photo Of The Day:

What Happened Today

DATE: _____

NOTES:

Photo Of The Day:

What Happened Today

DATE: _____

NOTES:

_____
_____
_____
_____
_____
_____
_____
_____
_____
_____
_____
_____
_____
_____
_____
_____
_____

Photo Of The Day:

What Happened Today

DATE: _____

NOTES:

_____
_____
_____
_____
_____
_____
_____
_____
_____
_____
_____
_____
_____
_____

Photo Of The Day:

What Happened Today

DATE: _____

NOTES:

_____
_____
_____
_____
_____
_____
_____
_____
_____
_____
_____
_____
_____
_____
_____

Photo Of The Day:

What Happened Today

DATE: _____

NOTES:

_____

Photo Of The Day:

What Happened Today

DATE: _____

NOTES:

_____
_____
_____
_____
_____
_____
_____
_____
_____
_____
_____
_____
_____
_____
_____
_____

Photo Of The Day:

What Happened Today

DATE: _____

NOTES:

Photo Of The Day:

What Happened Today

DATE: _____

NOTES:

_____
_____
_____
_____
_____
_____
_____
_____
_____
_____
_____
_____
_____
_____
_____
_____
_____
_____
_____

Photo Of The Day:

What Happened Today

DATE: _____

NOTES:

Photo Of The Day:

What Happened Today

DATE: _____

NOTES:

_____
_____
_____
_____
_____
_____
_____
_____
_____
_____
_____
_____
_____
_____
_____

Photo Of The Day:

What Happened Today

DATE: _____

NOTES:

_____
_____
_____
_____
_____
_____
_____
_____
_____
_____
_____
_____
_____
_____
_____
_____
_____

Photo Of The Day:

What Happened Today

DATE: _____

NOTES:
_____
_____
_____
_____
_____
_____
_____
_____
_____
_____
_____
_____
_____
_____
_____
_____
_____

Photo Of The Day:

What Happened Today

DATE: _____

NOTES:

_____
_____
_____
_____
_____
_____
_____
_____
_____
_____
_____
_____
_____
_____
_____

Photo Of The Day:

What Happened Today

DATE: _____

NOTES:

_____
_____
_____
_____
_____
_____
_____
_____
_____
_____
_____
_____
_____
_____
_____
_____
_____
_____

Photo Of The Day:

What Happened Today

DATE: _____

NOTES:

Photo Of The Day:

What Happened Today

DATE: _____

NOTES:

_____
_____
_____
_____
_____
_____
_____
_____
_____
_____
_____
_____
_____
_____
_____
_____
_____
_____

Photo Of The Day:

What Happened Today

DATE: _____

NOTES:

_____
_____
_____
_____
_____
_____
_____
_____
_____
_____
_____
_____
_____

Photo Of The Day:

What Happened Today

DATE: _____

NOTES:

_____
_____
_____
_____
_____
_____
_____
_____
_____
_____
_____
_____
_____
_____
_____

Photo Of The Day:

What Happened Today

DATE: _____

NOTES:

_____
_____
_____
_____
_____
_____
_____
_____
_____
_____
_____
_____
_____
_____
_____
_____
_____

Photo Of The Day:

What Happened Today

DATE: _____

NOTES:

_____
_____
_____
_____
_____
_____
_____
_____
_____
_____
_____
_____
_____
_____
_____
_____
_____

Photo Of The Day:

What Happened Today

DATE: _____

NOTES:

Photo Of The Day:

What Happened Today

DATE: _____

NOTES:

_____
_____
_____
_____
_____
_____
_____
_____
_____
_____
_____
_____
_____
_____
_____

Photo Of The Day:

What Happened Today

DATE: _____

NOTES:

Photo Of The Day:

What Happened Today

DATE: _____

NOTES:

_____
_____
_____
_____
_____
_____
_____
_____
_____
_____
_____
_____
_____
_____
_____

Photo Of The Day:

What Happened Today

DATE: _____

NOTES:

_____
_____
_____
_____
_____
_____
_____
_____
_____
_____
_____
_____
_____
_____
_____
_____

Photo Of The Day:

What Happened Today

DATE: _____

NOTES:

_____
_____
_____
_____
_____
_____
_____
_____
_____
_____
_____
_____
_____
_____
_____

Photo Of The Day:

What Happened Today

DATE: _____

NOTES:

_____
_____
_____
_____
_____
_____
_____
_____
_____
_____
_____
_____
_____
_____

Photo Of The Day:

What Happened Today

DATE: _____

NOTES:

_____
_____
_____
_____
_____
_____
_____
_____
_____
_____
_____
_____
_____
_____
_____

Photo Of The Day:

What Happened Today

DATE: _____

NOTES:

_____
_____
_____
_____
_____
_____
_____
_____
_____
_____
_____
_____
_____
_____
_____

Photo Of The Day:

What Happened Today

DATE: _____

NOTES:

_____
_____
_____
_____
_____
_____
_____
_____
_____
_____
_____
_____
_____
_____
_____
_____
_____

Photo Of The Day:

What Happened Today

DATE: _____

NOTES:

_____
_____
_____
_____
_____
_____
_____
_____
_____
_____
_____
_____
_____
_____

Photo Of The Day:

What Happened Today

DATE: _____

NOTES:

_____
_____
_____
_____
_____
_____
_____
_____
_____
_____
_____
_____
_____

Photo Of The Day:

What Happened Today

DATE: _____

NOTES:

_____
_____
_____
_____
_____
_____
_____
_____
_____
_____
_____
_____
_____

Photo Of The Day:

What Happened Today

DATE: _____

NOTES:

_____
_____
_____
_____
_____
_____
_____
_____
_____
_____
_____
_____
_____
_____
_____
_____
_____

Photo Of The Day:

What Happened Today

DATE: _____

NOTES:

Photo Of The Day:

Made in the USA
Middletown, DE
23 April 2019